Barb

DOLL COLLECTOR'S HANDBOOK

by

A. Glenn
Mandeville

Marl
Davidson

Priscilla
Wardlow

Gary R.
Ruddell

Published by

Hobby
House
Press

Hobby House Press, Inc.
Grantsville, Maryland 21536

Photographic credit. Thanks to the following photographers:

Photographs by A. Glenn Mandeville appearing on pages:
Front Cover, 1, 3 (bottom), 5-18, 20-36, 59-69, 84, 87-88, 92-94

Photographs by Scott Glushien appearing on pages:
3 (top), 42-48, 50-58, 85

Photographs by Kevin Mulligan appearing on pages:
73-74, 76, 78-81, 83

Front Cover: This nostalgic reproduction #1 Barbie doll from 1994 is just as charming as the real thing, but there is a major difference in value.
Title Page: Day-To-Night Barbie doll in 1985 was a busy, "Gold Card" carrying executive.
Table of Contents: Bob Mackie Gold, issued in 1990, was the first doll in the series. 1959 #1 vintage Barbie doll with mint face.
Back Cover: This #1 Barbie dressed display box doll is the ultimate rare collectible.

Barbie® Doll Collector's Handbook is an independent study by authors A. Glenn Mandeville, Marl Davidson, Priscilla Wardlow, and Gary R. Ruddell, and published by Hobby House Press, Inc. The research and publication of this book were not sponsored in any way by the manufacturers of the dolls, the doll costumes, and the doll accessories featured in this study. Photographs of the collectibles were from dolls, costumes, or accessories belonging to A. Glenn Mandeville, Marl Davidson, and Joe Blitman, at the time the picture was taken unless otherwise credited with the caption.

In order to capture the greatest detail of the dolls and accessories in the photographic process, the dolls and accessories will appear a different size than in real life.

The values given within this book are intended as value guides rather than arbitrarily set prices. The values quoted are as accurate as possible but in the case of errors, typographical, clerical, or otherwise, the authors and publisher assume no liability nor responsibility for any loss incurred by users of this book.

Hobby House Press, Inc.
1 Corporate Drive
Grantsville, Maryland 21536
1-800-554-1447

ISBN: 0-87588-480-6

TABLE OF CONTENTS

ABOUT THE AUTHORS

A. Glenn Mandeville
Antique & Collectible Dolls

A. Glenn Mandeville is regarded among doll collectors and dealers as an expert in identifying and appraising modern dolls. He is a staff writer and pricing editor for *Barbie® Bazaar* magazine. Mandeville's expertise is reflected in his regular television, newspaper, and magazine reports on dolls as well as his twenty plus years in the doll business. He has also authored the acclaimed *Doll Fashion Anthology* book series featuring teen fashion dolls. Other authored books include: *Sensational '60s, Alexander Dolls Collector's Price Guide (Volume I and II), Contemporary Doll Stars,* and *Ginny...An American Toddler Doll.* Contact Mr. Mandeville at: 380 Dartmouth Court, Bensalem, PA 19020   (215) 638-2561 • (215) 638-0105 FAX • E-mail: bkwanabe@aol.com

Marl B. Davidson
Marl & B

Marl B. Davidson is celebrating her 10th anniversary in 1997 as owner of Marl & B (formerly Marl & Barbie), one of the largest Barbie doll dealerships in the world. A formidable Barbie expert, Marl has appeared on many TV shows, has been interviewed by innumerable publications worldwide, and has written articles for such publications as *Collecting Figures, Millers Market Report,* and *Doll Reader.* Together with Joe Blitman, she co-produces 15 shows and sales specializing in Barbie dolls all over the country.

Marl is able to manage her growing business and still spend time with her family by making sure that family members attend her Barbie doll shows in their area. Look for Marl's new book release *Barbie Doll Structures and Furniture* in Fall 1997. Contact Mrs. Davidson at: 10301 Braden Run, Bradenton, FL 34202 (941) 751-6275 • (941) 751-5463 FAX • http://wwwauntie.com/marl

Priscilla Wardlow
NRFB Queen

Priscilla Wardlow has collected Barbie dolls and accessories since 1988, with a focus on NRFB vintage clothing and dolls. Priscilla has served as a competition judge at the national Barbie convention, is a past president of the After 5 Barbie Club of Minnesota, and served as co-chair of their mini-convention. She appeared with Twiggy in Mattel's 1996 My Fair Lady infomercial, as well as on other television programs in the U.S. and Japan. A graduate of Saint Olaf College and Harvard Business School, Priscilla lives and works in the Los Angeles area and travels the world in search of Barbie dolls. You may contact Ms. Wardlow at: 1200 Laurel Street, Pasadena, CA 91103 (818) 395-7690 • (818) 395-7890 FAX E-mail: nrfbqueen@aol.com

Gary R. Ruddell
Hobby House Press, Inc.

Gary Ruddell is the publisher and president of Hobby House Press, Inc., the Collector's Book and Video Source. Celebrating its 55th anniversary in 1997, Hobby House Press is the world's largest publisher of books devoted to dolls and teddy bears. Contact Mr. Ruddell at: 1 Corporate Drive, Grantsville, MD 21536 (800) 554-1447 • (301) 895-5029 FAX • wwwhobbyhouse.com

Treasures from Childhood – Starting Young

by Gary R. Ruddell

Publisher of Hobby House Press, Inc.

Girls love Barbie dolls.

Never Removed From Box (NRFB) condition is the cat's meow for adult doll collectors, but the wrong standard to hold youngsters to. A fashion doll is not a fashion doll unless one can dress and undress her and "Play Barbie Dolls"! So the question is, can a child bond with the Barbie doll and yet collect Barbie dolls?

Absolutely! Children at a young age can be taught good play values and respect for special playthings. The following technique can be used by a parent or a grandparent on children from the age of three up to teenager!

Break dolls into two groups — play dolls and collector dolls. Play dolls are those that can be dressed and undressed while collector dolls are those that are kept in glass protected cases or on high shelves. Regardless of the type of doll, involve the child in the opening and examination of the doll, clothing, and accessories. Encourage the child to notice detail and always add the appropriate "oohs and ahhs". Then, using a doll record keeping system (like the *Doll Record Book*), record all information about the doll: when the doll was received, for what occasion, who gave the doll, what items came with the doll, and how much the doll cost. Take a picture of the doll and then another of the child holding the doll. Both pictures should be placed in the *Doll Record Book*. Now you have an itemized collec-

tion list, critical doll information, and a special memory album of your child and their playthings.

Reinforce good play activities! Aid the play process by providing a carrying case. The child needs to know that after play time is over, the doll must be put away in her/his original state. That means that the doll and accessories are always put back together as a unit. Then have a special place in a child's room where play dolls reside.

Ask your child to share the fun and fellowship of special doll play. Parents, grandparents, and other friends can share in tea parties or other special play activities. Dolls can be taken on vacations which not only reinforces proper handling, but provides recreation time

5

Barbie dolls provide hours of interactive play.

for the child in transit or when vacation activities are limited. Taking dolls on vacation also provides special time for the child and parent to play dolls together.

Take a child shopping when she has saved gift money or allowance. Ask what dolls, she would like to add to her play collection. Ask if she would like to buy another copy of a special doll — in case her favorite needs rest and relaxation! Try to keep extra copies in NRFB condition and under the control of the adult.

Open a world of imagination by having children take their favorite Barbie dolls to school for show and tells or incorporate them into a school project. Remember, Barbie doll offers a world of opportunity and experience. She has been an astronaut, airline stewardess, pilot, rock star, career woman, veterinarian, pioneer...the opportunities are endless.

When a child has learned the play value and the steps to protect and preserve their plaything, then they are ready to take the next step and share fellowship with others. Find other adult collectors with children about your child's age and invite them to join a special children's Barbie collector club. Approach your local toy or doll store and ask if the children can meet at their shop. Perhaps, even ask the shopkeeper to carry some merchandise that encourages child collecting. Toys of childhood are the most popular collectibles for grown-ups!

Never pressure children to keep playing with dolls. When they grow older and leave dolls for a while, carefully pack up and save both the play Barbie dolls and the collector Barbie dolls. Do not give away the collection and memories that you and your child have created together. When they are ready to resume doll collecting they are reintroduced to their special treasure of childhood and have a record of special memories!

Remember Barbie doll collecting is fun and exciting for all involved!

GUIDELINES FOR CHILDREN & COLLECTOR DOLLS

Rule #1 — Make collecting fun!

Rule #2 — A child can only play with the collectible dolls when an adult is present.

Rule #3 — A child's dressing and undressing of collector dolls should only continue if the child is playing "nicely" with the doll.

Rule #4 — There are always lots of "oohs and aahs" of exclamation over the doll, costumes, and accessories.

Rule #5 — When play time is over, the doll must be returned to its original box with all proper clothes and accessories back in place.

Rule #6 — Maximize **Rule #1**!

CHAPTER 1

The Romance of Barbie Dolls
by A. Glenn Mandeville

Growing up is a time of change in a girl's life. Dreams of a first formal, the very first date, and other special occasions demand a whole realm of experience, confidence and an exciting wardrobe. Looking for a role model with experience and confidence could be a challenge, unless a girl knows Barbie...

For the past 38 years the Barbie doll has helped young ladies make the transition from pigtails to ponytails and onto the hip-hop and retro styles of today! The Barbie doll, designed in the mid '50s and intro-duced at Toy Fair in 1959, illustrated the Hollywood post World War II glamour to an entire generation of little girls. By the early '60s, the harsh, overly sophis-ticated styles of the '50s had given way to more feminine yet classic styles. Little girls loved playing with Barbie doll who now sported a clas-sic Bubble Cut hair style like America's First Lady and had the most gorgeous wardrobe. Barbie and her enticing world inspired many a

child during a time of transition. The extraordinary story of a beautiful girl's wonderful life was exciting to the Baby Boom generation.

As the British Invasion forever changed the world of fashion and music, Barbie doll went MOD in up to the minute London's Carnaby Street inspired fashions that were hip, groovy

A factory mint 1959 number one Barbie doll in front of her original box. She has her pink skin tones!

This brunette number one Barbie doll models the 1959 outfit Easter Parade.

and fab! In the '70s fringed suede and granny dresses were perfect for Peace Marches and as the decade closed, a new Superstar Barbie danced under a twirling Disco Ball! The '80s saw Barbie doll as a "Gold Card" carrying executive, yet still remaining glamorous as a veterinarian, an astronaut, and a rock star with her very own band! In the '90s Barbie doll has starred in classic film roles as well as having careers as a fire fighter, a chef, and a teacher.

Yes, the Barbie doll has represented a glamorous future for three generations of preteen girls who have adopted the famous Mattel motto, "We Girl's Can Do ANYTHING, right Barbie?". Through playing with Mattel's famous teenage fashion model doll, as Barbie doll was billed in 1959, a child can pretend to be a bride, a ballerina, an astronaut, or a teacher. In the late '50s and early '60s, Barbie doll showed an entire generation there were choices about the future. Be it a belle on a plantation or a registered nurse, Barbie doll could always be counted on to be a leader.

The first Barbie fashion booklet, packed with the dolls, showed the exciting ensembles available in 1959.

Ken doll was a cheerful chef in this wonderful early '60s fashion.

Barbie doll explored the world of careers as a registered nurse.

Barbie doll was head cheerleader at Willows High!

Barbie and Ken dolls were astronauts in the mid '60s!

During the '60s Barbie doll attended a State College, was a fashion editor, sang at benefit performances, was a student teacher and also a head cheerleader and drum majorette! Besides all of that she also found time to be a Candy Striper volunteer, travel to foreign countries dressed in native costumes, and perform classic fairy tales in a little theater group! Being a stewardess for several different airlines and then eventually a pilot, gave little girls a glimpse into a limitless future. During the mid '60s Barbie and Ken dolls took their first ride in outer space complete with flags to plant on the moon!

Starting in the early '80s, Black Barbie and Hispanic Barbie dolls led the way to dolls sold domestically that now represent virtually every ethnic guise imaginable. If you are Irish, Swedish,

Japanese or from Kenya, every little girl can now build a positive self image based on her ethnic background.

The success of the Barbie doll is because she represents not only the present, but the limitless future. Girls admire the positive traits and accomplishments of Barbie. No mountain is too tall to climb with a constructive role model, like Barbie doll, at your side!

Always living an active lifestyle, Barbie doll has resided in her very own Dream House, had her own Fashion Shop, moved into a Magical Mansion and has always had a spectacular wardrobe that was tailored from the finest fabrics with matching accessories. Yes, "The Barbie Look, the Fashion Look", for almost 40 years has kept Barbie doll at the cutting edge of style with designers such as Oscar de la Renta, Bob Mackie, Escada, Calvin Klein, Nicole Miller, Donna Karan and Ralph Lauren offering up stylish ensembles for the girl on the go.

Despite all the outward appearances of being a fashion icon, Barbie doll has always found time for her family and friends. In fact, it was the Barbie doll who broke racial play doll barriers with black friend Christie in the late '60s. Along with, best friend

The late '60s gift set "Barbie Loves The Improvers" showed how fashion had gone MOD!

A super rare 1967 Black Francie doll. The doll is being offered again for 1997!

Midge, Mod cousin Francie, friend P.J., and boyfriend Ken, Barbie has shared her most exciting adventures through not only hardcover books, but Fan Club magazines, comic books, record albums, paper dolls and now CD ROM's as well! Always current, Barbie doll today is state of the art. Even her television commercials use the very latest in computer generated animation. Barbie doll is more realistic than ever to a whole new generation of young fans!

Advances in manufacturing have made an entire genre of Barbie dolls that can talk via a home computer, pose more realistically than ever

Continued on page 19.

The perfect early '70s couple!

Live Action Christie
showed where the action
was in 1971.

The beat got turned around in 1977 with Superstar Barbie and Ken dolls.

Doctor Barbie doll treated all her patients in style in 1988.

U.N.I.C.E.F. Barbie doll (1990) was the first doll to be offered in four ethnic versions.

Western Barbie, Ken, and dog Turquoise, '90s style!

Who better to be an All American Beauty Queen than a 1991 Barbie doll?

before, and perform gymnastic stunts with ease! Fashions in all price ranges allow the child or collector to create a customized wardrobe. Well themed play settings can place Barbie doll under the sea with aquatic animal friends or on the stage performing classic ballet. Barbie doll in the late '90s is better than ever and just about everyone wants to be a part of the ever changing "World of Barbie"!

Starting right from the beginning in 1959, many adults realized the quality and workmanship that went into making Barbie doll the most fashionable doll ever! Rich silks, warm velvets, attention to detail and accessories were not overlooked by doll collectors. Others, who were children at the time, marveled at the craftsmanship and the excitement of the Barbie doll. They lovingly treasured and tended to each tiny hankie or gold compact with pride. Slippers with real pom-poms, pearl drop earrings and tiny charm bracelets were carefully stowed away after each play session. Details such as real zippers and silk lined purses are fond memories for many of today's collectors who played with vintage Barbie dolls as a child.

In the mid '80s, Mattel realized that there was a market for the adult collector with highly detailed dolls in a price point above the play doll line.

Barbie Collectibles (formerly known as Timeless Creations) is the Mattel division devoted to the adult Barbie doll collector of today. Offering not only the finest in runway quality fashion designs from Mattel staff designers and high profile fashion names; nostalgic versions of past editions of Barbie doll are offered as well. In 1994, the Number One Ponytail Barbie doll reproduction led the way to other ponytail dolls being featured along with the coveted 1965-66 Bendable Leg Barbie doll and Barbie doll's cousin Francie in her rare black version!

For the collector whose dolls are just a memory, these Nostalgic reissues can recapture a precious moment from the past or teach a valuable lesson on preserving the dolls of today. Collectors can choose from the regular line of Barbie doll and her sisters Skipper, Kelly and Stacie, and all of her friends, or the collectibles line of a world of high fashion! Dolls offered exclusively by mail through Barbie Collectibles or as store specials/exclusives only enhance the thrill of choosing which dolls will be added to a growing collection.

Barbie doll collecting is big business, but a fun business with some dolls increasing in value when they are discontinued. This, however, is not the main reason to collect Barbie dolls as most collectors will gladly state. It is the fun, i.e. the friendships at your local Barbie doll club, the chats on the Internet, and the exchanges of information at doll shows, that make the hobby so united in its focus to enjoy the passion of Barbie doll collecting. While the trend toward hoarding multiples of "hot" dolls is fading, sales are better than ever as collectors embrace the many offerings available to them in such diverse locations as the local

This Nostalgic reproduction number one Barbie doll from 1994 is just as charming as the real thing!

pharmacy to upscale boutiques! Exclusive dolls made specifically for the foreign market also add to the collecting frenzy. Almost everyone has a different reason for collecting, but the bond is still the same. A quality doll that has a nostalgic past, an up to the minute present, and a brilliant future is just so enticing to children and adults alike.

Barbie doll collecting is something the entire family can enjoy as many men and boys find the exciting lifestyle of Barbie and Ken doll irresistible as well. After all, Barbie doll has owned just about every top selling luxury car in the world as well as her own yacht and private planes! The thrill of the hunt for vintage and current Barbie doll items is irresistible to the whole family. Vacations can be planned around trips to major conventions and doll shows or museums devoted solely to Barbie doll collecting with plenty to do for the whole family.

Why not visit your local toy retailer today and see what you are missing, or if you are already a collector, view the latest offerings in all tastes and price ranges. Barbie doll is here and now as the past, present and future unite to produce an American pop legend. Make Barbie doll and her world a part of YOUR world today!

Pop culture themes such as Baywatch Barbie and Ken dolls keep the surf hopping.

Barbie doll represented the United States in the 1996 Olympics!

CHAPTER 2

A Fashion Doll is Born and Lives the Stylish Life
by A. Glenn Mandeville

Few three dimensional objects can impact society as much as a fashion doll. Fashion dolls have told a tale for centuries of what styles each generation dared to consider high fashion.

In the mid '50s, the children of post World War II parents were growing up. Since their parents had been preoccupied with The Great Depression and a global conflict, it was doubtful that they knew what it was like to be a teenager free from the stress of survival. Who was going to show these new found teenagers the way? What idols would exist for them to emulate?

Mattel Toys in the early 1950s was a small but growing business. With Ruth and Elliot Handler at the helm, the stage was set for exciting new things to happen. The Handler's daughter, Barbara, had an intense interest in paper dolls. On a trip to Europe Ruth's interest in a German doll named Lilli was sparked. This doll was a bit risque, but still had a certain innocent quality about her. Missing, however, was

the concept of additional accessorized fashions as the doll was really a novelty item. The Handlers fell in love with the idea of creating a fashion doll with accessories and upon their return to the United States began formulating plans to make the "Barbie" doll, named for their daughter, a reality.

Designer Charlotte Johnson was hired to begin work on the most tasteful of wardrobes for the Barbie doll. The

1959 was the debut of Barbie doll. Her white irises and arched brows stand right out.

The number two Barbie doll was the same except for the holes in her feet.

The third Barbie doll in 1960 had blue irises and curved brows.

doll and her clothing was to be manufactured in Japan under the highest quality control. The first dolls, now so highly prized, did not look like what Barbie would eventually become. After some refinements as well as resistance on the part of toy buyers, the doll became a hit where it really mattered...with little girls everywhere. After four changes in just two years, the Barbie doll finally looked like the girl next door.

At first, the idea was that the Barbie doll would have no identity except that which the little owner would bestow upon her. The first television commercials sang of "Some day I'm going to be exactly like you...till then I'll make believe that I am you." Little girls LOVED the Barbie doll and immediately wanted to know more about her. Soon the doll took on the identity of many of the movie star and television teenagers of the day and became her own persona. Girls were enthralled! Here was a perfect teenager to whom they could look up to and admire! Soon Barbie doll had a boyfriend Ken and a best friend Midge! A Fan Club was started on a national level and children were encouraged to start their own local chapters. It was the beginning of the Barbie doll era...and it is still going strong.

Fashion and pop culture which once evolved slowly now changed almost yearly. Already the designs of the late '50s were outdated as the turbulent '60s began. Mattel revised Barbie doll into the popular look of the early '60s teenager. Looking the

By 1961, the fourth Barbie doll looked all American and so did her boyfriend Ken!

The Bubble Cut was the latest hairstyle in 1961. Barbie doll wears it beautifully.

The 1962 Ponytail doll had a softer look and a range of hair and lip colors.

picture of class and grace, Barbie doll's wardrobe reflected the Camelot years (Kennedy White House) of white gloves, pearl necklaces, and bouffant hairstyles.

In 1965, the music and pop culture scene changed dramatically with a new emphasis on youth. Overnight Barbie doll changed to a sleek new look with a one length bob hairstyle and new Bendable Legs! Changes were rapidly occuring.

Barbie has a new look! The news was everywhere as Mattel launched the new Twist 'N Turn Barbie in 1967. She was better than ever, and now had a more "youthful" face, real rooted eyelashes and long, swinging straight hair! Her wardrobe consisted of the new

"mini skirts" worn with long coats and high boots! Innovations, such as Talking Barbie and her friends P.J. and Christie, gave girls a chance to play teenagers as never before.

The '70s ushered in fashions based on a country in conflict but when it was over, Barbie and Ken dolls took to the Disco floor with yet another revision in Barbie doll's face mold — a mold that is still used today on many dolls. Superstar Barbie and Ken entered the decade in grand style as the '80s brought a new sophistication and glamour, an enticement for the adult collector.

By the '90s, Barbie was a mainstream fashion doll to both children and

Continued on page 31.

A 1964 Swirl Ponytail doll with rare platinum hair and white lips.

Bendable Leg Barbie was new for 1965. Her hair was a short bob.

The 1966 Bendable Leg Barbie had vibrant make-up and lush, fuller hair.

The new Twist 'N Turn Barbie doll of 1967 had a more youthful face and long straight hair.

Barbie doll talked in 1968 with a pull string on her back!

Barbie doll's new flip hairstyle in 1969 was considered hot!

Living Barbie in 1971 wore a softer look for a new decade.

This dazzling new face mold for Superstar Barbie in 1977 is still used today.

The 1980 Black Barbie was an instant hit with girls!

In 1988, the first Happy Holidays Barbie was introduced and thus began the collectors market!

adults. Store specials and even limited editions of play dolls would beckon to those of all ages who loved fashion dolls. The Happy Holidays series, beginning in 1988, would prove to be one of the best selling and popular dolls of all times.

The addition of Bob Mackie designer Barbie dolls in 1990 would also catapult Barbie doll to a fashion leader. Each year the Bob Mackie series continues to be a popular item in the Barbie Collectibles line-up.

Mattel designers are among the best in the world. Many have fashion backgrounds that include the great design

houses of America and Europe. Each year, the Classique Collection features a different Mattel designer. Dolls only available by mail also feature designs by in-house as well as outside top designers. Never in the history of Barbie doll have there been so many choices.

Today it is hard to name a department store that does not have a Barbie doll exclusive. The so called play line of dolls is as interesting to adults as it is to children while the dolls marketed for the adult collector are coveted by many a child! Yes it is the world of the fashion doll and Barbie doll is at the top and has been for almost 40 years!

Bob Mackie Gold, issued in 1990, was the first doll in the series.

Teen Talk Barbie doll in 1992 used a brand new head mold seldom seen today.

The 1992 Mackie Neptune's Fantasy is a favorite of many collectors.

The Great Eras collection debuted in 1993 with Gibson Girl Barbie doll.

FAO Schwarz Silver Screen Barbie doll from 1993 is highly collectible.

A very popular doll of 1994 was the elusive Gold Jubilee Barbie doll.

From Walt Disney World to the neighborhood pharmacy, one can find the latest and the best in designer couture.

The Barbie doll has been the symbol of pop culture and stylish fashion
since 1959. No other doll has lasted so
long, or so fashionably, at the top!

Few dolls can claim to have been
the object of so many literary works, but
one thing is clear — Barbie doll is the
spokesperson for generations of children and adults alike who think that she
represents what fashion is all about...the
mirror of our culture and the symbol of
the American Dream.

Collectors love the
1995 FAO Schwarz
Jeweled Splendor.

The 1995 Nostalgic reproduction of Solo in the Spotlight brings back happy memories!

CHAPTER 3

Barbie Doll Talk

compiled by Hobby House Press, Inc.

The popularity of Barbie dolls has created new phrases and many collector-inspired acronyms. Learn the Barbie doll language!

Shorthand

AG............................American Girl

AO ....All original

BA...................................Bent Arm

BC ....Bubble Cut

BL ....Bendable Leg

CT ....Closed toe shoes

DOTW ....Dolls Of The World

DSS ....Department Store
Special (same as Exclusive)

EXC or Excellent ....Excellent
condition, some use or slight
wear but it looks brand new.

FH ....Flocked Hair (Ken)

FQ ....Fashion Queen

G or Good ....Good condition,
the doll has been played with
and needs restoration.

GWTW ....Gone With The Wind.
(Refers to the famous movie.)

HTF..............................Hard To Find

LDSSASE or LSADSE ....Long
double-stamped self-addressed
stamped envelope.

LE ....Limited Edition

MIB ....Mint In Box.
Factory mint doll and original box.
Box has been opened, shrink wrap
broken, tape cut, or box unglued.

MIP.......................Mint in Package.
Clothes & accessories have not been
removed from original packages.

MNB or MNP ....Mint No Box or
Mint No Package. Mint doll
without its box or package.

MOC ....Mint on Card. Clothes &
accessories have not been removed
from their original packages.

NRFB ....Never Removed
From Box. On older dolls: box has
never been opened, shrink wrap
broken, tape cut, or box unglued.
On newer dolls: the shrink wrap
has not been cut open or damaged,
or the glue on the box has not
been pulled apart.

OF...Outfit

OO ....Original Outfit

OT.............Open-toe shoes or mules

P or Poor ....Poor condition, doll
restoration not feasible

PH ....Painted Hair (Ken)

PT ....Ponytail

PTR..............................Palm to rear

PTS..............................Palm to side

SASE ....Self Addressed
Stamped Envelope

SG....................................Sunglasses

SL ....Straight leg

SS ....Swimsuit

TNT ....Twist 'N Turn,
first launched in 1967

VG or Very Good ....Very Good
condition, played with, needs
some work.

#1 Ponytail, the 1959 original Barbie doll, white irises, blue liner, holes in feet.

#2 Ponytail, same 1959 original Barbie doll, but no holes in feet.

#3 Ponytail, the 1960 Barbie doll, blue irises, more gently curved eyebrows.

#4 Ponytail, the 1960 Barbie doll with new vinyl used for her body.

#5 Ponytail, the 1961 Barbie doll, new hair texture, hollow, lighter-weight body.

Key Phrases

Barbie® Bazaar..........The Barbie doll collectors magazine. This is a Mattel licensed magazine.

Ballerina Style Arms ....In addition to the up and down movement, arms also move away from the sides.

Book Box ....The box opens like a book with a hinge.

Children's Collection ....Collector Edition Barbie dolls designed to appeal to the youngest collectors.

Collector Edition ....Barbie dolls that come in showcase packaging. These dolls have specially selected facepaint, skintones and hairstyles and wear highly detailed ensembles.

Contemporary ....Refers to Barbie dolls and outfits issued between 1981 and present.

Couture Period..............Barbie dolls made between 1964-1966.

Customized Doll ....Dolls created exclusively for a specific store.

Disco ....Barbie era 1977-1979 when the disco dance outfits abounded.

Exclusive ....Barbie doll created exclusively for a specific store. Mattel refers to this as a customized doll.

First Market ....Available from merchants or catalogs.

International Barbie ......Barbie doll made outside of the U.S. under a license with Mattel.

Internet Access ....Barbie dolls, information and fellow Barbie doll collectors accessed through a PC. Some key names to remember: rec.collecting.dolls; rec.collecting; rec.toys.misc.

Limited Edition ....Produced in more limited quantities, these Barbie dolls feature fine fabrics and unusual details that set them apart from all other Barbie dolls.

Living Arms ....Joint at both the elbow and wrist.

Mark..............................The letters, numbers of names impressed on the back of the head or body

Mattel, Inc. ....The company who created Barbie doll in 1959 and has nurtured her ever since.

Miller's...........................An independent magazine for Barbie doll collectors.

Mint & Complete ....Pristine outfit and all accessories in mint condition.

Mod ....Barbie dolls made between 1967-1972.

Nostalgia ....Barbie dolls made for collectors starting in 1994.

PAK ....Budget mix-and-match garments that were sold separately.

Secondary or Collector's Market ....Dolls that are no longer available from the manufacturer through merchants. The dolls are available from doll dealers or collectors.

Shoe Box ....The lid comes off exposing the Barbie doll and accessories to view.

Timeless Creations........Mid-1980's thru 1996 Mattel Division that marketed Barbie dolls for collectors. Now known as Barbie Collectibles

Vintage ....Refers to Barbie dolls and outfits issued between 1959 and 1972.

Window Box ....Look-in style often with a cellophane panel.

BARBIE® DOLL'S FAMILY & FRIENDS

* All of the names present in this chart are protected names.
The legal protections were left off for the readability of this chart.

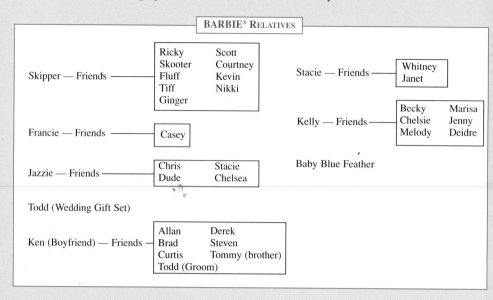

BARBIE® RELATIVES

Skipper — Friends —
Ricky, Scott
Skooter, Courtney
Fluff, Kevin
Tiff, Nikki
Ginger

Francie — Friends —
Casey

Jazzie — Friends —
Chris, Stacie
Dude, Chelsea

Todd (Wedding Gift Set)

Ken (Boyfriend) — Friends —
Allan, Derek
Brad, Steven
Curtis, Tommy (brother)
Todd (Groom)

Stacie — Friends —
Whitney
Janet

Kelly — Friends —
Becky, Marisa
Chelsie, Jenny
Melody, Deidre

Baby Blue Feather

BARBIE® FRIENDS

Midge	Jamie	Tracy	Dee Dee	Bopsy	Deyon	Tara Lynn
Christie	Steffie	(Bride)	Diva	Becky	Nia	Kayla
Stacey	Kelley	Miko	Whitney	Belinda	Nikki	
P.J.	Cara	Dana	Teresa	Kayla	Kira	

HEART FAMILY
Mom, Dad and Babies (Boy & Girl)
Grandma and Grandpa Heart 1986
Baby Cousins
Kenny, Kevin (black), Honey,
Janet, Melody, Millie

HEART FAMILY NEIGHBORHOOD KIDS
Wendy, Gillian, Doria, Darrin,
Pleasance (hispanic), Tawny (black)

BARBIE® FOREIGN FRIENDS

Carla
Valerie
Chantel Goya
Flora
Ellie
Living Eli (Japan)
Tulie Chan (Japan)
Skip Chan (Japan
Noel (Japan)
Stephanie (Japan)
Sophie (Japan)
Wayne Gretsky
Bob (Rio version of Ken)
Bobbi BeBobs
Alexia

KOREA
Kotbie
Danbie

BRAZIL
Lia
Diva
Vicky
Bobby

EUROPE
Marina
Laura

INDIA
Monica

BARBIE® CELEBRITY LICENSED FRIENDS

Twiggy
Julia
Miss America
Donny Osmond
Marie Osmond
Jimmy Osmond
Kitty O'Neill

Kate Jackson
Cheryl Ladd
Debbie Boone
Kristy McNichol
Buffy & Mrs. Beasley
M C Hammer

Barbie® Doll's Family & Friends

* All of the names present in this chart are protected names.
The legal protections were left off for the readability of this chart.

International Barbie®

Royal Barbie	German Barbie	Japanese Barbie	German Barbie
Parisian Barbie	Icelandic Barbie	French Barbie (Can Can)	Polynesian Barbie
Italian Barbie	Canadian Barbie	Russian Barbie	Chinese Barbie
Oriental Barbie	Korean Barbie	Puerto Rican Barbie	Dutch Barbie
Scottish Barbie	Mexican Barbie	Artic Barbie	Kenyan Barbie
India Barbie	Russian Barbie		Mexican Barbie
Eskimo Barbie	Nigerian Barbie	**Reissues of:**	Indian Barbie
Spanish Barbie	Brazilian Barbie	Parisian Barbie	African Barbie
Swedish Barbie	Ghanian Barbie	Eskimo Barbie	
Irish Barbie	Malaysian Barbie	Scottish Barbie	
Swiss Barbie	Czechoslovakian Barbie	Spanish Barbie	
Japanese Barbie	Australian Barbie	English Barbie	
Peruvian Barbie	Native American Barbie 1-4	Italian Barbie	
Greek Barbie	Norwegian Barbie	Irish Barbie	

Outer Space Barbie® Friends

Sun Spell
Moon Mystic

Barbie® Babies

Barbie Baby-Sits Baby	Skipper
Sears Baby-Sits Baby	Baby Sitter Courtney
Baby Sitter Skipper	Heart Family Cousins
Black Baby Sitter	Mertwins

Barbie® Pets

Honey	Tahiti	Turquoise	Blinking Beauty	Butterfly (Stacie)
Midnight	Fluff	Sun Runner	Sachi	Western Star
Dallas	Prancer	Star Stepper	Honey	Keiko (Whale)
Pups of Beauty	Dog 'N Duds	Snow Ball	Wags	Nibbles
Dixie	Dancer	Zizzi Zebra	Tiffy	Goldie
Prince	Beauty	Ginger Giraffe	Chelsie (Skipper)	

Barbie® Pet Animals w/O.F.'s or Sets

Put Ons and Pets — black Poodle	Jamie's grey Poodle
Put Ons and Pets — Afghan	Jamie's white Poodle
Put Ons and Pets— white cat	Skipper's Terrier
Scottie — Skipper's Dog Show	Kevin's Dalmation
Dog — Tutti's "Me and My Dog"	

Other Mattel Fashion Dolls

Lori 'N Rori	Asha	Davy Crocket	Phoebus
Angie 'N Tangie	Shani	Mary Poppins	Quasimodo
Nan 'N Fran	Nichelle	Tinker Belle	Creuell DeVil
Heart Family	Jamal	Peter Pan	Ursula
(Mom, Dad, Girl, Boy,	Cinderella	Wendy	Ariel
Baby and cousins)	Prince Charming	Alice	Snow White
	Belle	Truly Scrumptious	Elvis
	The Beast	Pocohantas	
Heart Family's	Sleeping Beauty	John Smith	
Grandparents	The Princess Jasmine	Nakoma	
Trueheart	Alladin	Kocoum	
(Heart Family Dog)	Pirate of the Carribean	Esmeralda	

CHAPTER 4

Tips on Collecting Barbie Dolls
by Marl Davidson

Starting a collection

The most important tip I can give to anyone who is starting their own collection is to have fun — if you remember that, the rest is a breeze!

With that in mind, trust me when I say the more you know about collecting the more you will enjoy Barbie dolls so, EDUCATE YOURSELF! It is your responsibility to know the who's, what's, where's, when's, and why's of what you are collecting. You cannot depend solely on the opinions and assumptions of others. There are virtually hundreds of ways for the novice Barbie doll collector to become a Barbie doll expert. It won't happen

overnight, but if you follow a few basic steps, it will happen.

1) Read, read, read and read some more. With the release of many, many books about every possible facet of Barbie doll collecting, anyone can learn anything they want to know. Start with what interests you the most, and go slow. Whether you are interested in vintage or contemporary items, you will find books that explain markings, editions, and issue years. Look for publications and price guides that will give you input on conditions and values. You will find that once you get a good solid foundation of knowledge

Barbie Doll Magazines

Barbie Doll Dealer List

the rest will come easier, and that's when the real fun begins. (See pages 85-86 for a listing of popular Barbie doll books.)

2) In all this reading don't forget to pick up publications, such as *Millers Market Report, Millers Collector,* or *Barbie® Bazaar* magazine. Released periodically throughout the year, these magazines prove invaluable in providing you with the most current information. This is your way of keeping abreast of what's new and what's hot. These magazines are also useful educational tools with articles of interest and price guides that show the ever fluctuating Barbie doll prices.

3) In the spirit of keeping up with ever changing prices, your most dependable resources are dealer lists. Send for several different lists, so that you can have a realistic idea about average costs of specific merchandise. Dealer lists also supply you with an outlook to the more popular dolls, how the market is progressing, and a resource to learn condition ratings and how that rating effects the price of a doll.

4) Go to shows — I can not emphasize this enough! There is no better way to learn than with hands-on experience. Show shopping gives you the opportunity to see exactly what prices and conditions can be expected, as well as letting you pick and choose your items. Shows also provide the opportunity to meet dealers and collec-

Barbie doll show scene.

tors, ask questions, and build friend-ships. Not only will you gain first hand knowledge on Barbie doll and her family but you will have fun doing it!

5) The Internet has proven to be a great source of information in the Barbie doll collectible world. There are information folders and chat rooms, where you can ask questions and talk to fellow collectors and deal-ers about all aspects of collecting. Web pages and sites also offer dealer infor-mation, specials, and a ton of tid-bits about your favorite hobby. A visit to the web can be a truly enjoyable adventure.

6) My last piece of advice is to join a local Barbie doll club. This puts you in direct contact with other Barbie doll lovers who will be a great source of knowledge. Plus they are guaranteed to understand your new found love of this 11-1/2 inch vinyl goddess, more than anyone else. Clubs always have the information on what's going on, where the shows are, who the best dealers are, and what to invest in.

Remember, an educated collector is less likely to be taken advantage of, and they will also know a great Barbie doll deal, when they see it!

How to stretch those dollars

Once you get started it's hard to find enough time in the day to look for and locate the things you want, not to mention trying to find enough money in your wallet. Here are some tips on how to make the most of your Barbie Doll Budget:

1) Give yourself an allowance and STICK TO IT — this is a Barbie doll collecting imperative. Once you've allotted yourself a specific amount, you can better plan your future purchases. If you are on a quest for a specific "something" don't settle for something else, hold out for the exact items you want. This also means buying the best you can afford, however, don't confuse quality with quantity — you want a collection you can be proud of, not a number to impress.

2) You can't collect it all so don't even put that type of pressure on yourself. If vintage is your love, stick with one or two specific eras (e.g. 1959-1964) or types of dolls (e.g. Ponytails, Bubble Cuts, American Girls or Twist 'N Turns). If the newer dolls are more your speed, try one or two of your favorite series (e.g. Happy Holidays or Bob Mackie dolls). Remember — the first in the series is usually the best investment.

3) Buy dolls that need some cleaning. Don't run from messy hair or lip rubs, and don't let (mildly) green ears or dirty bodies scare you off. All of these common Barbie doll afflictions can be easily

1966-1970 Vintage. Mod Era Collection.

Contemporary dolls from the Happy Holidays Collection.

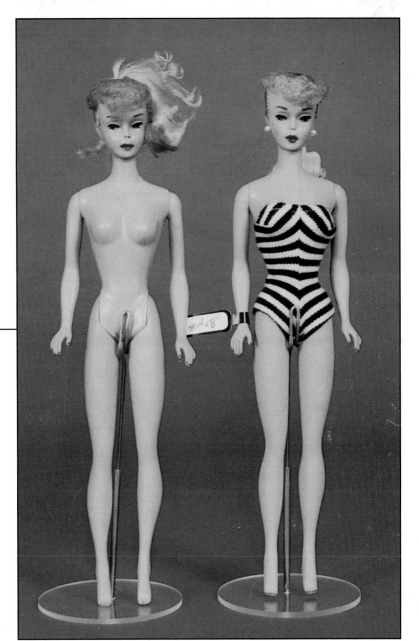

1960 #5 vintage Ponytail dolls. Restorable *(left)* and Restored doll *(right)*.

remedied. Your choices are simple — learn how to fix and clean up dolls from the various videos, articles, and books available to you, or send the doll to one of the many available restorationists. If you decide to go the restora- tionist route, make sure to choose one with a good reputation, ask for references, and check this person out before you send out any merchandise. Most often you can buy and fix up a doll for less than it would cost to

1967 vintage Francie before hair restoration.

1967 vintage Francie after hair restoration.

buy the same doll in the condition you desire. For the beginner who is attempting to fix doll afflictions, purchase a less valuable doll to practice on before attempting your favorite or best investment!

4) Buy from reputable dealers. This will save you so much time and money you won't believe it. You won't have to worry about not receiving merchandise, wrong heads on bodies, being ripped off, or common oversights that the less experienced dealers just don't notice. All reputable dealers offer a return privilege and are quite knowledgeable. But most importantly, they have a reputation to uphold, and they want your business. Don't be afraid to ask for references and check them out. Be wary of any dealer who won't explain their return privilege. Be a savvy shopper!

48

How to create a great collection

A collection is only as great as the collector thinks it is. Remember that you are collecting for your enjoyment.

1) Collect what you like! Everything in your collection doesn't have to be the hottest, most limited, or the most expensive item, it only has to be enjoyable to you! If you see a $5.99 Barbie doll that really catches your eye, don't think about investment potential, think about how much joy she will bring you. Remember, Barbie doll collecting is fun!

2) The second rule is DISPLAY IT! Let's be honest, half the fun of having a collection is showing it off. People don't just want to hear about it, they want to see it too. The display of a collection is a demonstration of not only its monetary worth but its emotional worth as well. Be a cautious and educated displayer by following the simple rules outlined in Chapter 7, *Tips on Preserving & Conserving Barbie Dolls.*

Saving and storing information will save you money

The following tips will help you to be a more organized, cost efficient, and responsible collector.

1) Insure your collection. Get a valid appraisal from a trustworthy source. This is the last thing on most collectors minds, but when you think about how much money you have invested, it is a logical step. Ask friends in the Barbie doll world which insurance companies they use and trust.

Tip: Make sure the insurance company understands box condition can be up to 50% of an item's value. Most companies don't understand this axiom and will not compensate you for box damage if the doll is seemingly still mint. This is especially true in cases of smoke and water damage.

2) Keep an up-to-date record of the time of purchase, price you paid, and individual photos of every Barbie doll in your collection. This will prove invaluable for research on pricing, collection worth, insurance purposes, and the resale of dolls.

3) Keep an ongoing, well organized inventory of your entire collection. This will help guard against theft, as well as make your collection more accessible. If you keep specific dolls in certain areas of your home, give each area a code and assign it to the items located there. Keep a second inventory copy away from your home.

4) If you think it's important, it probably is. No one will ever know everything there is to know about Barbie doll collecting, as new details are revealed everyday. It is important though, to have references that are available at the exact moment you need them. Use a file cabinet or a computer and file/record any information you feel is pertinent to your collection.

Marl's Barbie doll collection is preserved in glass cases.

CHAPTER 5

How Collectors Grade the Condition of a Barbie Doll

by Marl Davidson

When it comes to grading conditions there are specific qualities that collectors look for when preparing for a purchase. There is a huge difference, however, in what a vintage collector seeks as opposed to a contemporary collector.

A vintage collector has to be on the look-out for more specific attributes such as:

- making sure the heads and bodies match
- knowing the difference between retouched and original make-up

- identifying methods and markings of dolls.

These attributes are necessary knowledge because of the limited number and age of vintage dolls.

Most contemporary collectors will tell you that there are only two important aspects of the newer collectible Barbie dolls:

- box condition
- appearance of the doll (if the doll and costume are pleasing)

Vintage

There are six major categories that influence vintage condition: hair, head, make-up, body, box, and accessories. The quality and presence, or lack thereof, determine condition as we know it.

Note: Subjects such as retouched make-up and re-styled hair are personal preferences to each individual collector. Whereas these items could never be what we are describing as mint (defined as factory perfect), if acceptable to a collector, and professionally done, it could command a rating as high as near mint.

1960 #5 vintage Barbie doll with perfect hair.

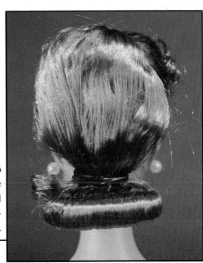

1961 #6 vintage Barbie doll with re-styled hair.

51

1966 Twist 'N Turn vintage Barbie doll with perfect hair.

The following information, will give you the necessary ingredients that make a MINT doll.

• Hair — Perfect hair has never been redone. For instance, with pony-tails the original top knot and bottom knot is still present with original rubber bands and hard curl. The 1966 and 1967 Twist 'N Turns would have the original bow and rubber band, no hair cuts, damaged hair, or missing plugs.

• Head — This item can be divided into three categories:

1. Neck — The neck can't have any splits or cracks and must be securely held onto the torso of the doll.

2. Ears — Ears must not have any green on them at all, not even the smallest dot.

3. Face — The face must first have perfect make-up (for description see section marked *Make-up*). There cannot be any missing pieces of vinyl, such as nose, chin, or eyelash nicks. Later dolls with rooted eyelashes cannot be missing plugs of eyelashes.

• Make-up — Make-up must be original and flawless — no rubs, chips, or fading. This includes all paint on the face of the doll (e.g. eyebrows, eyes, eyelashes, blush and lips) as well as any other paint anywhere else than the body (e.g. fingernails and toenails). If any part of the doll has been retouched it cannot be considered mint.

1959 #1 vintage Barbie doll with mint face.

• Body — This category includes skin color, arms, legs, and torso. Skin color should be even. In cases of #1's, #2's, and #3's, where fading is normal (although, an original pink tone is more desirable) a consistent fade (even to a pure white) is totally acceptable and does not devalue a doll. Arms and legs must fit into sockets perfectly, without any

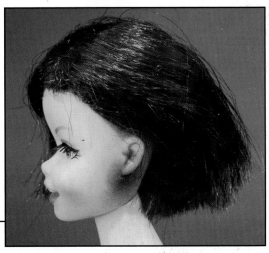

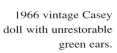

1966 vintage Casey doll with unrestorable green ears.

1962 Bubble Cut vintage Barbie doll showing poor head and mint head.

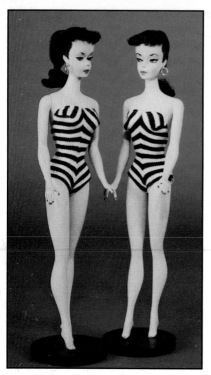

1959 #1 vintage Barbie doll. Pink body and faded white body.

missing fingers/toes and all finger-nails/toenails (when applicable) should be painted. Dolls with bendable legs must have thighs that are right at the hip joints, both knees must click, and no tears in or wires poking through the vinyl. Torsos must not have scratches, busts cannot have dents or pin pricks, and the neck knob (when applicable) must be in tact and sturdy.

Note: Items such as: mold marks, bow legs, and transitional parts may not be as desirable, however they are completely normal and do not decrease the value of an otherwise flawless item.

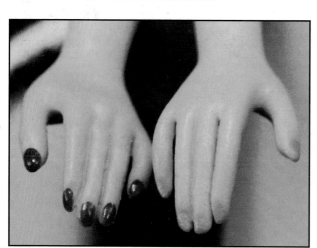

1961 Bubble Cut with mint nails and poor nails.

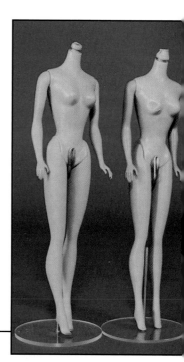

Vintage pony-tails. Mint body and poor body.

Vintage box in poor and mint condition.

1959 #1 vintage Barbie doll. #1 box with accessories in mint condition.

• Boxes — Boxes must be perfect without any rips, tears, rubs, or fading. Both endflaps must be present as well as the original box liner.

• Accessories — This includes (when applicable) earrings, stand, wrist tag, booklet in original cello, sunglasses, original outfit, and shoes. Each accessory must be present and in pristine condition.

Contemporary

Contemporary dolls are easier to grade as they are newer and most often still in their original condition. They have not had to overcome the years of wear and tear of vintage dolls, however that does not detract from the contemporary doll's desirability. Condition on these items are divided into three categories: box condition, doll condition, and accessories.

1995 contemporary Starlight Waltz from the Ballroom Beauties Series. Damaged box.

The making of MINT contemporary dolls is as follows:

1. Boxes — The condition of the box must be as perfect as possible. The box cannot be dented, creased, or ripped in any manner. There can't be any spots or fading, and front display cello (when applicable) must be in tact and unflawed (this means no scratches, or holes, and cello must be connected to the box). Also, the doll must be securely bound to the liner.

2. Doll Condition — For dolls in or out of the box, this includes hair, head, make-up, and body. Hair must be in original condition. Head must be on the body and fit snugly. Make-up must have no rubs or fading. The body must have legs, arms, and torso, all in working order.

3. Accessories — This includes (when applicable) original outfit, shoes, jewelry, wrist tag, booklet, stand, brushes, and other specific specialty items that are primarily available only with specific dolls. These must be present, pristine, and in proper working order.

Remember, there are no guarantees and taste is subjective. However by following these basic guidelines, you will have a good idea of what condition a Barbie doll is in, and therefore be able to make an educated judgment of its worth. The following is a simplified chart which you can use to grade dolls of all conditions:

1996 contemporary Bob Mackie Sun Goddess. Mint doll out of box.

1993 contemporary Western Stampin Barbie Gift Set with complete accessories.

Mint...Factory flawless (in or out of box), pristine

Near Mint...Not played with and shows no signs of wear but not as crisp as mint

Excellent...Still very nice, but slightly played with

Very Good...Played with, but still has some life left in it

Good...This item was "well-loved," but still has some value

Fair...Very played with, but has more than one redeeming quality

Poor...Extremely played with, but has at least one redeeming quality

NOTE: Always remember that vintage Barbie dolls sold for $2.99 in 1959 and contemporary Barbie dolls were all produced on an assembly line and were toys made specifically for children. Therefore, you will find manufacturing variances — perfection is elusive!

CHAPTER 6

Factors That Determine the Value of your Barbie Doll

by Gary R. Ruddell

1. **Love.** With Barbie doll enthusiasts it's love at first sight! We fall in love with her face, her hair, her fashions, her accessories or memories of play with Barbie! Removing Barbie dolls from the box can reduce the value of your Barbie doll by 50%! Memories of Barbie doll play are priceless. Some Barbie doll collectors buy two models, one to play with and the other to leave in NRFB condition.

2. **Condition.** The state of the Barbie doll is crucial to establishing a value. Refer to Chapter 5, *How Collector's Grade the Condition of Barbie Doll*, for more detailed descriptives on condition.

3. **Supply and Demand.** Remember the collector axiom — buy cheap and sell high! The supply and demand of Barbie dolls reacts to the normal dynamics for these terms. Because of the number of different doll models being

This Number One Barbie dressed display box doll is the ultimate rare collectible and valued at over $10,000!

released each year and the 1,000 plus previous model introductions, one must discuss supply and demand by the individual Barbie doll.

Vintage Barbie doll supply was fixed when manufacturing ceased. Many of the Barbie dolls were played with and thus the supply of NRFB Barbie dolls or better grade dolls is more limited. With the addition of many passionate collectors, the demand for vintage and contemporary dolls has increased. Collectors must turn to the secondary market, the collector market, to obtain such dolls. The collector value keeps increasing as long as sufficient demand is in place to pay the higher collector values. In unusual situations, such as when a rare or unusual doll becomes available, dolls may fetch a premium due to demand. Special event introductions or auctions can produce unusual pricing events because a collector will purchase emotionally. Great care should be exercised in buying just after a big value increase. Initial demand may inflate the collector value above what a more settled demand market may support.

Speculation exists when sellers

This rare sidepart Barbie case and Swirl Ponytail doll from 1965 are worth about $2,500.

Think Mink! A Sears exclusive mink coat and 1966 American Girl Barbie were high-fashion in the mid-'60s. Current value $2,000 MIB. Today, Barbie dolls are fashionable without furs.

and collectors buy up additional dolls greater than their needs. They speculate that the collector value will increase and they hold dolls to sell at that higher value. If the values do not increase, the supply becomes greater as speculators dump their excess stock. This can depress collector values.

Likewise, if the supply of Barbie dolls from Mattel is greater than the demand for that doll model, then merchants will discount the price in order to move the dolls. The astute collector tracks demand for their dolls and buys or sells accordingly.

4. **Popularity.** Barbie dolls experience fads. The increased interest in Mod Era Barbie dolls (1967-1972) has caused the value of these dolls to escalate.

A Rare Japanese American Girl Barbie doll models an outfit exclusive to Japan, circa 1967. Value for both — $2,600.

The 1986 Billy Boy Barbie doll was the first department store special collectors took note of. Value today is $175 up.

The 1989 Lincoln Center Silver Jubilee Barbie doll is treasured at $1,500!

The now discontinued Great Eras Collection started in 1993.
Flapper Barbie doll a 1993 release (featured above) currently sells for $125.

The 1995 International Happy Holidays Barbie doll is very desirable to American collectors...valued at $125.

Barbie dolls are made in substantial quantities but if demand is strong enough a premium value is placed on the doll. Collectible Barbie dolls and department store exclusives have been quite popular. While many covet special doll models the collector marketplace value may inhibit a rising demand for particular dolls.

5. **Desirability.** When the collecting passion first strikes, the collector is rarely discriminating. What pleases a collector today, may not please the collector tomorrow. We grow and we change. Collectors evolve and become more discriminating. They look for and desire Barbie doll models that represent sought-after fashions, occupations or a return to the nostalgia of yesteryear. Collectors yearn for perfection and the unusual. They want something that others covet.

6. **Total Originality.** Collectors as they evolve become more discriminat-

ing. In the beginning a collector sometimes buys quantity over quality. Once the wallet dictates a prioritization of expenditures and discrimination, total originality becomes a model that collectors pursue. They are less inclined to accept restored dolls. They want Mattel manufactured examples with no flaws! They buy quality over quantity. A premium is therefore put on desirable dolls that represent the ultimate in Barbie doll collecting. Sometimes Barbie dolls in NRFB condition are harder to find as so many enthusiasts played with their dolls. Because of the premium of originality, NRFB collectors should carefully examine the "total" package.

Barbie dolls are fashion plates. Collectors expect original clothing. Replaced clothing reduces the value of a Barbie doll. Be careful to ascertain if there has been migration of dolls' clothes and accessory coloring dyes with the dolls' skin.

The hair should be original set.

All accessories should be present and the box must be intact. The total originality of the set matching Mattel production is the expectation of collectors.

The 1996 Toys R Us Pink Ice Barbie doll retailed for $150 and featured a silk shantung dress.

1994's 50th Anniversary Porcelain Barbie doll can still be found at retail.

CHAPTER 7

Tips on Preserving a Barbie Doll Collection

by A. Glenn Mandeville

Fortunately for Barbie doll collectors, the care of a doll collection is relatively easy with a few effortless to follow guidelines. When the restoration of vintage items is the challenge, modern technology is there to help!

CAUTION: Never perform an action which cannot be reversed. If the action is irreversible, try the procedure on a less expensive doll first or consult with an authority.

Many collectors enjoy dolls that are never removed from the box. Others rejoice in touching and posing their Barbie dolls. There is no right or wrong way to collect but there are certain practices that will allow you to enjoy your collection to the fullest as well as preserve the value for future generations.

Vintage dolls (dolls manufactured from 1959 to 1972) are starting to age

This '60s doll has "Green Ear" from the metal in the earrings. It can be successfully restored.

Flea market finds like this doll can be made to look like new!

and require delicate care to maintain or restore that feeling of "just like new". Surface dirt can be gently removed with soap and water. Should ground in dirt be a problem, there are products advertised in Barbie collector magazines that will safely remove ground in soil without damaging facial paint or delicate plastic joints. When in doubt, leave heavy duty restoration such as repairing a talking mechanism or rejoining a limb up to a professional. Many people advertise that they restore vintage Barbie dolls. Be sure to check references and get an estimate in writing. Most of these people are highly skilled individuals and well worth the price. For the do-it-yourself crowd, the number one consideration is patience!

Missing make-up can be retouched with concentrate artist acrylic paints. Use a light touch, a fine brush and then "set" the paint by holding the face in a pair of tongs over a steaming pot of boiling water for at least a minute. If you omit this step, the paint will eventually run and ruin the doll.

Ponytails can be redone with a little practice. Wash the hair in a detergent based cleanser followed by a fabric softener. A fine tooth comb will separate the hair and allow you to see the longer "wrap" strand that goes around the ponytail at the crown. Comb the ponytail into place, secure with an orthodontic rubber band and then wrap the longer strand around the rubber band. Lift the underside of the rubber

Some collectors have built in elaborate displays that protect their dolls.

Rare vintage items displayed behind glass make an enchanting presentation.

band with a bobby pin and pull the wrap strand through.

The end of the ponytail can be rolled on a permanent wave roller and then dipped in boiling water to "set" the roll. Practice on flea market finds first. If you luck onto a valuable doll such as a #1 at a low price, it is better to send the doll out for a professional refurbishing unless you are very skilled at restoration. The important thing to remember is that unless the repair is virtually undetectable, it hasn't been done correctly. Note all restoration to a doll in a notebook so that future owners will be aware of what has been done to your dolls.

The collector of contemporary Barbie dolls also has a responsibility to preserve the dolls in mint condition.

The following advice applies if you are keeping your dolls in the box. Buy dolls in boxes that are in excellent condition but avoid being overly critical of normal box wear. Display your collection on shelving out of direct fluorescent lighting as this can fade both the dolls and the boxes. Make sure the temperature is within normal ranges as extremes can result in the growth of mold or insect infestation. (Both are very rare under normal household conditions). When storing dolls that are boxed, use acid free materials and layer the dolls so that air can circulate around them.

Many collectors today are opening the newer dolls and displaying them for their enjoyment as well as part of the decor of one's home. Many dolls are packaged so that you can enjoy them without opening them, but others really should be taken out of the box to enjoy. Some of the same rules apply to keep your dolls in mint condition. Display the dolls in a curio cabinet behind glass away from children and pets. Make sure that the temperature in the room is constant, i.e. avoid high humidity and extremes in heat or cold. Remember that dust and sunlight are the only real enemies of modern dolls. Consider built-in cabinets for an extensive collection and rotate dolls a few times a year from storage to display.

None of this means that you have to keep your dolls under glass permanently. A holiday display where dolls are out in the air temporarily does no damage if properly displayed out of direct light and the reach of children and pets. In fact, plastics actually thrive in areas where air is circulating so don't be afraid to enjoy your collection with a few precautions. Advanced collectors have mastered the art of enjoying their dolls in a responsible setting.

Aside from holiday displays, don't overlook entrance halls, (domes with dolls inside are a very effective first impression), dining room tables, book-case units, children's rooms and entertainment centers all come alive with the addition of a few Barbie dolls. What better way to enjoy a classic movie than with some Hollywood themed Barbie dolls mixed into the environment! Elementary school-aged children can be taught the joys of caring for treasured objects, often a lost art in hectic times. The care of a Barbie doll collection is a perfect starting point for many lessons on the joys of tending to fine things.

There is no purpose in collecting dolls unless you are going to enjoy them. For some, that means keeping dolls and outfits perfectly preserved in the original packaging. For others, it means built-in or purchased cabinets and elaborate displays.

There is no one way to enjoy your Barbie doll collection. With a little common sense and these practical conservation tips, there is no reason why your Barbie doll collection cannot give you a lifetime of enjoyment! Maintaining your collection and sharing restoration and display tips with other collectors is just one more way to make your Barbie doll collection a joy forever!

CHAPTER 8

Where Can I Find Barbie Dolls?

by Priscilla Wardlow

The short answer is "Everywhere". There are countless sources, so it pays to be vigilant, always on the search.

Before you go shopping, become well educated. Buy and study reference books which apply to your collecting interests. Not only will this help you save money and frustration by knowing what you are looking for and how much it should cost, but it will also prevent you from buying dolls with mismatched parts and incomplete outfits. You will also be ready to recognize a true bargain when you see it.

Read first, buy second. Reference books will help you shop intelligently.
(Miniature books by Rebecca Brosdahl.)

Let's Go Shopping — Finding Barbie
Out in the World

Toy and department stores are excellent sources of current Barbie dolls. In addition to the generally available play and collectible dolls, some stores, such as Toys 'R Us, FAO Schwarz, Bloomingdale's, Target, Wal-Mart, Service Merchandise, et al, have special "store exclusive" dolls which are quite collectible.

Doll shops typically offer a wide selection of current collector Barbie dolls, including store specials from other parts of the country, international dolls, and the current Mattel col-

Dialing for dolls! The phone can be great for mail order, locating shops, answering ads, and bidding in auctions.

lectible line. Doll shops may offer vintage Barbie merchandise as well. Check the yellow pages of the phone book to find doll shops, either in your own area or while traveling. And when traveling internationally, go prepared with translations of "dolls" and "toys" to speed up your search.

Doll shows are a particularly exciting place to find dolls. You can find ads for upcoming shows in *Barbie® Bazaar, Miller's Market Report,* and *Doll Reader®,* as well as in local newspapers. Barbie shows typically have a wide variety of new and vintage merchandise. Several promoters have show series that travel around the country, and many people plan vacations around attending these national shows. Watch, too, for Barbie conventions and mini-conventions, which typically open their salesrooms to the public at the close of the convention. And don't forget general doll, bear, and toy shows. They can be good places to find a Barbie bargain hiding among other dolls and toys.

Vintage Barbie dolls and accessories may also be found at antique shops, flea markets, thrift shops, and garage sales. This is where studying your reference books can pay off — there are still great things to be found if you know what you're looking for. Recently, a #1 was found among a bunch of '90s dolls in a thrift store bargain bin!

Shopping from Home — Bringing Barbie to You

There are a number of options for building your Barbie collection without leaving the comfort of your home. Whichever options you pursue, be sure to check references before you send money and be sure that the items you are buying are well-identified and fully described. If you are dealing with a new supplier, you may wish to place a small initial order to ensure that you and your dealer/store have similar definitions of condition of dolls and boxes, timely order processing, and other satisfactory transaction requirements.

Mail order has been the backbone of Barbie collecting for many years and dealers' lists have been the mainstay of mail order. Both contemporary and vintage dolls and clothing can be purchased from dealers' lists. Check through magazines such as *Miller's, Barbie® Bazaar, Doll Reader®,* and *Contemporary Doll.* In both display ads and classifieds, you will find notations such as "Lists for LSADSE," which translates to, "Sales list available if you send a large, self-addressed, double stamped envelope." Major dealers, such as Joe's, Marl & B, Kitty's Collectables, and Sandi Holder's Doll Attic, offer subscrip-

Check the fine print for Barbie doll ads.

tions to their lists. Subscribe if you are interested in receiving lists promptly and regularly. A hint for shopping from lists — order quickly for the best selection, but don't be afraid to call about an item after a list has been out for some time. Often a dealer will have duplicate items available or will have received new merchandise since the publication of the list.

Doll shops and department stores are also excellent sources for current dolls by mail order. Store exclusives may often be ordered directly from the original source, such as FAO Schwarz, Bloomingdale's, and Macy's. Both doll shops and mail order dealers will be happy to take your pre-order for

new releases from Mattel, assuring that you will receive your dolls as they arrive from the factory and saving you from running around looking for them once they are out. Each year, Happy Holidays dolls seem to go through a period of scarce supply. By pre-ordering from a dealer, you can have the Happy Holidays come to you, rather than have to chase it from one place to the next.

Auctions are a fun (and sometimes nerve-wracking) way to add to your collection. Few things are as exciting as chasing an item in an auction and emerging the winner! McMaster's and Scherzer's are two popular, reputable Barbie doll auctions. In both cases, you can place your bids by mail or telephone in advance of the auction date. McMaster's holds their auction in person so you can be there to raise your bids and experience "auction fever". They will also bid for you, so you can enjoy the auction from home. Scherzer's conducts a telephone auction, where you can call in and raise your bids. As with any kind of auction, be sure to ask questions about your item before the auction so you understand exactly what you are bidding on. Also, set some personal guidelines so that you don't get carried away and forget your budget. Bargains can be found. Don't be afraid to start low and work up.

Barbie dolls are also available on television. QVC runs regular Barbie programs, where dolls and related items are offered for sale. Mattel also features periodic infomercials show-casing new dolls. The Classique series, Barbie as Scarlett, Barbie as My Fair Lady, and the Bob Mackie Jewel Essence series have all been presented through half-hour infomercials over the past few years.

You can also go shopping for Barbie in cyberspace! Search the Internet under key word Barbie or go directly to Mattel's Barbie doll web site at: http://www.barbie.com.

There are bargains to be had in cyberspace, as it affords individual collectors an inexpensive forum for marketing their dolls. As mentioned above, however, be sure to check references before conducting transactions by computer. While the vast majority of sellers on the Internet are honorable and reputable, the anonymity of the computer interface does shelter a few shady individuals.

The Personal Way to Find Barbie Dolls

If you collect vintage dolls, it can be to your benefit to spread the word about your interest. Word of mouth among family and friends may just unearth a treasure from someone's attic. Many collectors have business cards printed which they can hand out to let people know that they are interested in buying Barbie dolls.

Advertising for wanted Barbie dolls can also be a successful, though pricey, way to uncover vintage collections. While newspaper and magazine advertising can be expensive, free local papers and bulletin boards can get the word out for you cheaply.

If you are looking for particular dolls or accessories, put together a "Want List" and distribute it to dealers and shops where you do business. While not all dealers can keep track of your wants, many will perform this service and help you find what you're looking for.

Finally, fellow Barbie collectors can be an excellent location source. Let your collecting friends know when you admire something in their collections — if they later decide to sell it or if they find another, they just may call you.

CHAPTER 9

Where and How Can I Sell Barbie Dolls?

by Priscilla Wardlow

Finding places to sell Barbie dolls can be a bit trickier than finding places to buy them, but there are many avenues available to an informed collector.

The Trade-Off — Speed, Effort, and Value

The fastest way to sell dolls is to a shop or dealer. Approach a dealer whom you know and trust and ask if he or she has interest in what you are selling. Typically, you will receive less than full retail value on your merchandise, but you may be able to sell everything you are offering with little effort for instant cash or credit. Only you can decide the trade-off between value and time that this method of selling entails.

A second way of selling is directly to collectors. This method may bring you more money, but requires considerably more time and effort. You can run ads in doll magazines and papers, sometimes at reduced rates if you are a subscriber. Two excellent publications that offer very reasonable classified ads are *Collectors United* and *Master Collector*. You can also publish your own list and offer it through ads, if you have a quantity of

Frenzied bidding at auctions may bring a high value for rare items.
(Miniatures by Rebecca Brosdahl.)

Doll shows combine social occasions with shopping.
(Miniatures by Rebecca Brosdahl, Michelle McCloskey, and Susan Miller.)

items for sale. This method requires that you be available to take orders and answer questions by phone or mail and that you are equipped for shipping merchandise across the country or the world.

You can also have someone represent you in selling your Barbie things, either through consignment or through auctions. Dealers who offer consignment services will mention this in their ads and lists. Auctions, either in person or by mail or phone, can be used for a variety of merchandise, but they are particularly good for rare items, since they reach a broad spectrum of collectors and give an opportunity to reach very high prices on desirable things. Both Scherzer's and McMasters are well-established auctions and there are new auctions being offered all the time.

Another way to reach collectors directly is by setting up a table at a doll show. Contact the promoter of an upcoming show to reserve and purchase space, then prepare your items for display, keeping in mind that you want things visible, well-described, and protected from pilfering. On the day of the show, arrive early to set up your table and to benefit from pre-show buying opportunities. An advantage of this selling method is that it requires a short, intensive time commitment, but you are dependent upon the schedule of shows in your area or those to which you can travel.

A third way to sell directly to collectors is to employ the Internet, either advertising on your own Web page or listing items for sale on electronic bulletin boards. If you go this route, be prepared to check your e-mail frequently and respond in a timely fashion to all inquiries. Things move fast in cyberspace, so you need to move fast yourself to be a good seller. Deals may also fall apart quickly, so be prepared to re-post the item and go on to the next person. Happily, since the costs of selling by computer are low and revisions to your list are instantaneous, it is easy to recover from incomplete transactions.

If you plan to sell Barbie dolls for a long period of time, you may wish to take a showcase or booth in an antiques or collectibles mall. Having a space in a mall allows you to display your items and sell them without having to be present.

Don't discount the value of word of mouth when selling items from your collection. Think first of your collecting friends. Those who are familiar with your collection and who have admired it, may be interested in adding items from your collection to their own.

Barbie doll on the Internet. Check out Mattel's Barbie web site online.

Tips for Selling:

- Be sure to describe your merchandise accurately. Point out any known flaws so that the buyer will not be disappointed. Identify items clearly as to condition and completeness. Post prices prominently if you are selling in person.

- Be realistic on pricing your merchandise. Contemporary dolls that are still available from retailers may have to be sold at a price less than what you paid. If you are selling vintage merchandise, recognize that price guides typically list NRFB prices and mint and complete prices. If your items are not mint, adjust the price down accordingly.

- Be prepared to answer questions regarding layaway payments and taking less than your posted price. It is a personal decision whether you wish to take payments over time as a service to your customers or whether you wish to discount.

- For mail order, explain your terms of business clearly. Is shipping included in the price? Do you take credit cards and checks, or only money orders? Is there a return privilege? (By advertising in most doll magazines, you are automatically offering a five-day return privilege.) When do you expect payment? How long will you hold merchandise while awaiting payment? And what method of shipping will you use?

- If you are selling through ads, lists, or cyberspace, be ready to provide references who can attest to your reputability. If you have never sold before, ask dealers from whom you have bought if they will vouch for your reliability in honoring commitments, sending payment, and following

Tips for Selling:

through with transactions. Once you have sold
a few things, ask your customers if they will
provide references.

- When selling at a show, don't forget to bring
  supplies to make your life easier and to help
  you be professional. Bags, receipts, change,
  and business cards are all necessary parts of
  selling in person. Consider your display methods
  and bring shelves, bins, or whatever might
  be helpful to show off your merchandise.

- Enjoy the process of selling! There are wonderful
  people to meet in the Barbie world and a
  customer today may become a friend tomorrow.

Barbie collectors enjoying their purchases after a Barbie doll show.
Left to right: Christy Conn, Christine Harper, Annette Givens, Laura Jicha, Kimberly Hayes,
and Rachel Oakley.

CHAPTER 10

Barbie Dolls Are the Talk of the Universe!

compiled by Hobby House Press, Inc.

You can maximize your access to Barbie doll information by following some simple steps. Create your own Barbie Doll Directory by examining the following data bases:

Barbie Doll Collector's Club

See page 96 for more information.

Barbie Fan Clubs started in the early '60s. Here Barbie doll is a member of the 1966 club!

Barbie Doll Books

The passion for Barbie doll information has spawned the publication of scores of Barbie doll books. Visit your local bookstore, a chain bookstore, a Barbie doll dealer, a doll specialty shop, or mailorder companies and find a book to help you!

Hobby House Press publishes or stocks over 40 different books on Barbie dolls and her friends! For a free catalog call 1-800-554-1447. Or visit our Barbie doll book web site at wwwhobbyhouse.com. You will be glad that you did! For with knowledge comes appreciation!

Recommendations for basic Barbie doll collector libraries:

Barbie Doll Boom Identification and Values
by J. Michael Augustyniak

An encyclopedia of collectible Barbie dolls 1986-1995 with values. Features over 800 dolls in full color. 144 pages. #N5050 $18.95

Barbie Doll Collector's Handbook
The ultimate tips handbook for starting a Barbie doll collection and having a lot of fun doing it! 100 color photos. 96 pages. #H5301 $12.95

Some Barbie doll books available today.

Barbie Exclusives Identification & Values, Vol. I
by Margo Rana
Wal-Mart, Sears, Disney, porcelain treasures and more Barbie doll store specials. 300 color photos plus collector values. 160 pages. N4873 $18.95

Barbie Exclusives Identification & Values, Vol. II
by Margo Rana
Toys 'R Us, Dolls of the World plus many more store specials complete with values. 300 color photos. Plus collector values. #N5049 $18.95

Barbie Doll Exclusively for Timeless Creations, Vol. III
by Margo Rana
Features color photos plus collectors values on Barbie dolls made for adults from 1986 thru 1996. 360 color photos. 160 pages. #H5296 $24.95

Barbie Doll & Her Mod, Mod, Mod, Mod World of Fashion
by Joe Blitman
Full color encyclopedia showcasing all vintage Barbie dolls and fashions 1967-1972 plus collector values. 575 color photos. 224 pages.#H5145 $26.95

Collector's Encyclopedia of Barbie Dolls & Collectibles
by Sibyl DeWein & Joan Ashabraner
This was the first book on Barbie dolls and is definitive on the 1959 thru 1976 period. 928 photos. 224 pages. #N2837 $19.95

5th edition, Doll Fashion Anthology & Price Guide
by A. Glenn Mandeville
The story of the evolution of Barbie dolls and other fashion dolls through photographs and choice collectors information. Collector values. Nearly 300 photographs. 216 pages. #H5035 $14.95

Having fun is the number one experience of collecting Barbie dolls. The friends that you interact with and meet at clubs, shows, or through the Internet, make Barbie doll collecting what it is — special and fun. Club meetings give you the maximum opportunity to see and handle Barbie dolls and related collectibles. To locate your nearest club, surf the Internet; consult *Barbie® Bazaar* and *Miller's* magazines; and visit doll shows.

In 1993 this Toontown Stacie was only available at Walt Disney World and Disneyland.

My Favorite Barbie Doll Stores or Dealers are:

Doll Dealers & Specialty Stores

You will find dealers and specialty stores fountains of knowledge on vintage and/or contemporary Barbie doll collectibles. You can be the beneficiary of their knowledge and tips. To find Barbie doll dealers browse *Barbie® Bazaar* and *Miller's* magazines; surf the Internet; and visit doll shows.

Vintage. To visit a vintage dealer, it is best to make an appointment. You may also shop with them via show, telephone, mailorder catalog, or Internet.

Contemporary. Many walk-in or mailorder doll specialty stores advertise in Barbie doll magazines (best source for store specials and/or exclusives). The Internet is also a growing specialty store source.

Here is a sampling of vintage and contemporary doll dealers:

Joe Blitman
Joe's
5163 Franklin Avenue
Los Angeles, CA 90027
(213) 953-6490 telephone;
(213) 953-0888 FAX

A. Glenn Mandeville
Antique & Collectible Dolls
380 Dartmouth Court
Bensalem, PA 19020
(215) 638-2561 telephone;
(215) 638-0105 FAX
E-Mail bkwanabe@aol.com

Marl Davidson
Marl & B
10301 Braden Run
Bradenton, FL 34202
(941) 751-6275 telephone;
(941) 751-5463 FAX
Web: wwwhttp://auntie.com/marl

Margo Rana
Margo's
2726 De La Vina Street
Santa Barbara, CA 93105
(805) 687-5677 telephone;
(805) 569-0088 FAX
Web: http://www.mastercollector.
com/dealer/margo.html

Priscilla Wardlow
NRFB Queen
1200 Laurel Street
Pasadena, CA 91103
(818) 395-7690 telephone;
(818) 395-7890 FAX
E-mail: nrfbqueen@aol.com

Sandi Holder
The Doll Attic
2488 Regal Drive
Union City, CA 94587
(510) 489-0221
(510) 489-7467 FAX
Web: http://users.aol.com/sandihb4u/
dollatic.htm
E-mail: sandihb4ue@aol.com

Alice Norman
Diamonds & Dolls
511 St. Louis Street
Springfield, MO 65806
(417) 866-8111
(417) 882-3497 FAX

Internet

Barbie dolls is a very active topic in cyberspace! You can find a growing number of Barbie doll web sites on the 'Net. Surf the 'Net and discover the resources that best fit your information desires.

Here are some select entries:

* Baddogs Groovy World
  (Craig Dawson) Information on
  Canadian Barbie dolls.
  http://www.interlog.com/-baddog

* Barbie Collectibles (Mattel Barbie
  Doll Homepage)
  http://www.barbie.com
  1-800-624-1456 to order via
  conventional telephone

* Hobby House Press, Inc.
  Barbie Doll Books
  wwwhobbyhouse.com

* Marl and B
  wwwhttp://auntie.com/marl.

* Margo Rana
  Margo's
  http://www.mastercollector.com/
  dealer/margo.html

* Compuserve has Collector's Dolls
  Forum (several conference rooms,
  some photo libraries and an
  auction).

* Prodigy has a bulletin board for
  exchange of information on
  Barbie dolls.

* Internet Usenet Groups have
  varying quantities of Barbie
  information traffic:
      rec.collecting.dolls
      rec.collecting
      rec.toys.misc.

Barbie Doll Magazines

The strength of the Barbie doll magazines are the multitude of Barbie dolls and collectibles which are featured in articles and advertisements. You can keep abreast of the current happenings in the world of Barbie dolls.

Barbie® Bazaar
The Barbie Doll Collector's Magazine
5617 6th Avenue
Kenosha, Wisconsin 53140
Published bi-monthly at $26.95 per year
(414) 658-1004; (414) 658-0433 FAX

Miller's
An Independent Magazine for
Barbie Doll Collectors
P.O. Box 8722
Spokane, WA 99203-0722
Published quarterly at $16.95 per year
1-800-874-5201; (509) 455-6115 FAX

Miller's Market Report
News, Advice and Collecting Tips
for Barbie Doll Investors
P.O. Box 8722
Spokane, WA 99203-0722
Published monthly at $24.95 per year
1-800-874-5201; (509) 455-6115 FAX

It's easy to sell interesting dolls like this 1990 Barbie Style doll done for Applause under license.

Shows

Getting together is one activity that Barbie doll collectors excel at! Shows provide enthusiasts with a chance to see and handle rare to common dolls up close as well as the opportunity to purchase many kinds of Barbie treasures from dealers and specialty stores. A huge benefit from attending shows, is the comradery that develops between collectors, dealers, and store owners. You have a chance to meet other people who share your love and passion for Barbie dolls!

Check out the calendars and ads in *Barbie® Bazaar, Miller's, Doll Reader®* and *Dolls* magazines as well as the Internet for show schedules. There is a Barbie Doll Convention held annually. The Barbie Doll Convention is hosted by a Barbie Doll Club at different cities around the United States. The 1997 event will be held: August 20-23, 1997 in San Diego, CA. For more information contact: Cynthia Chapman at (619) 660-8107. The registration deadline for this event is long past, but you may inquire about a public day.

Barbie Dolls & Friends Sized Up

Barbie and female friends ....11-1/2"

Supersize and Pretty Dreams Barbie ....18"

My Size Barbie ....36"

Francie and Casey ....10-7/8"

Skipper, Skooter, Ricky ....9"

Teen Skipper ....9-1/2"

Kelly and Teacher kids ....4-1/4"

Stacie, Todd, Janet, Whitney, etc. ....7-3/4"

Ken and male friends ....11-3/4"-12"

Tiny babies for Dr. Barbie, Babysitter ....2-5/8"

The ethnic version of Walmart's Superstar Barbie doll from 1993 is very sought after on dealer's sales lists.

Selling dolls like this 1992 Toys R Us Radiant in Red is easy at doll shows.

The Official Barbie Collector's Club 1997 Charter Membership Doll —
Grand Premiere Barbie doll.

The Official Barbie Collector's Club^{SM}

The Official Barbie Collector's Club offers a convenient and fun way for Barbie doll devotees to become more involved in Barbie doll collecting. With the purchase of a 1997 charter membership from Mattel, Inc., club members receive a membership kit complete with a pin, exclusive Date at Eight™ fashion, binder, newsletter (Premiere issue) and an official guide to collecting fashion through the years. Members will also receive a membership card, quarterly newsletters, and an invitation to purchase the club exclusive doll, Grand Premiere™ Barbie® doll.

A 1997 charter membership can be purchased for $39.99. For more information contact:

The Official Barbie Collector's Club
P.O. Box 182227
Chattanooga, TN 37422-2227
1-800-491-7503

— NOTES —